The Northport Arts Coalition presents ...

Poetry Path
A Walk in the Park

Cover photography by Tom Langton

Poetry Path ~ A Walk in the Park

Copyright © 2024 Northport Arts Coalition

All rights reserved.

Published by Red Penguin Books

Bellerose Village, New York

ISBN 978-1-63777-562-2

No part of this book may be reproduced in any form or by any electronic or mechanical means, including information storage and retrieval systems, without written permission from the authors, except for the use of brief quotations in a book review.
All individual works are copyrighted to the writers and artists.

The Northport Village Poetry Path was born as a dream. A dream to bring poetry off the pages of books and out of the confines of reading rooms. A dream to bring poetry into the open air for the entire Village to enjoy. And it was clear this dream was shared.

When Northport Arts Coalition put out the call, the Long Island poetry community responded wholeheartedly with fifty-six submissions. Twelve were chosen to be displayed for the path's inaugural year and three were named honorable mentions to be included in this book. The art that accompanies them was created especially for each poem by Long Island artists.

Wherever you are when you read these poems, let your imagination take you to the beautiful harborside park where they're displayed. Let yourself savor them as you stroll slowly from one to the next to the next, shaded by centuries old trees and serenaded by seabirds. Let them take you to new places and fill you with new thoughts.

Of course, we hope you'll have the opportunity to experience the Northport Village Poetry Path in person. Who knows, perhaps you'll be inspired to create your own poem for consideration for the 2025 Northport Village Poetry Path collection.

See you in the park!
Amy Connor
Executive Director
Northport Arts Coalition
www.NorthportArts.org
NorthportArtsCoalition@gmail.com

MISSION STATEMENT AND HISTORY

The mission of the Northport Arts Coalition is to inspire and support artists and to promote collaboration and connection within our island community. We embrace all creative disciplines, welcome diversity, and volunteer in the endeavor of planning and sponsoring artistic gatherings. We aspire to bring the arts in all their forms to a varied audience through entertainment, education and participation.

NAC was founded in 1998 by a group of artists dedicated to giving themselves and other artists a way to bring their art to the public. They met once a week at the Northport Historical Society and in private homes. In 1999 NAC was incorporated and received non-profit status. It has since grown into an organization of volunteer arts professionals who work to bring the arts in all their forms to both Northport and the wider community. NAC runs programs in several venues, including NAC Presents! at Northport Library, Friday night Happenings on Main Street free concerts in Northport Park every summer, monthly Poets in Port poetry readings year round, an annual Northport ArtWalk event throughout Northport Village, the annual Art in the Park Festival, and a year-round rotating art exhibit at Daniel Gale's Northport real estate office. In keeping with NAC's mission to bring the arts to the community, all of our events are free to the public so that cost won't be a limitation on who can access the arts.

Board of Directors

Amy Fortgang Connor - Executive Director
Manny Falzon - Music Director
Sandra Cialo - Newsletter Coordinator and Webmaster
Linda Trott Dickman - Secretary, Poetry and Spoken Word Director

Joyce Kilmer wrote, "I think that I shall never see a poem as lovely as a tree."
The Northport Arts Coalition invites you to enjoy beautiful poetry among the magnificent trees and glorious natural surroundings of the Northport Village Park.

The Northport Arts Coalition thanks the following people and organizations for their support and sponsorship:
Mayor Donna Koch
Village of Northport Board of Trustees
Trustee Meghan Dolan, Commissioner of Parks

Northport Village Poetry Path Exhibit Sponsors:
Linda and David Dickman
Mary Sheila Morrisey
Nolan Funeral Home
Lauren and Dan Paige
James P. Wagner

The Northport Village Poetry Path is sponsored in part by generous grants from:
The Huntington Arts Council
New York State Council on the Arts
PSEGLI

Foreword

I saw my first Poetry Path in Bellingham, Washington on a visit. I was immediately drawn in and explored the path and the website where the path's story was told. I contacted the library, and the creators of the path and the contest to see how it was done.
(https://thepoetrydepartment.wordpress.com/2012/08/24/sue-boynton-poetry-walk/)

I walked the path, and hoped I could raise excitement for it in the 2012 school year. It was presented to School Principals, Arts Administrators, anyone who would listen, and always it was a polite response, followed by no action. One fourth grade student actually wrote a 'persuasive letter" to convince others that the idea was a good one. Natalie Perusse is now in the High School.

When I mentioned it to Amy Connor, Executive Director of the Northport Arts Coalition, the idea was met with more than a polite response, it was met with immediate support of poetry and a quest for grants and actions to make it happen. As a result of the original idea, shared vision and the acquiring of the necessary funds and support, the poetry path is happening!

Welcome to this, our first poetry/art collaboration! The poetry came first, the artists then interpreted the poems. Here are the fruits of our labor, the poems, the art that was paired with them and the joy of seeing them together in a place where all can enjoy them.
Thankful for Amy's diligence in applying for and receiving the grants.

~ Linda Trott Dickman, BSE, MLS, MFA, NYS Woman of Distinction 2023

You are Northport

By Paula Curci *Artwork by Kate Kelly*

We called you Wading Place Creek.
You came from the Matinecock nation.
You lived off the land,
and fished in the bay,
before the English cow ranchers
settled in the meadow.

We called you Village Park.
You were a ship builder
rigging schooners,
and racing steam liners
with pilot-boats
before your yard became a park.

We called you Vernon Valley.
You met your gal on Main Street
wearing your stylish Trilby.
After you stepped off the trolly
and headed to the Sweet Shop
to order two egg creams.

We called you Highland Park.
You shouted verses in the rain,
after giving your nickels
to Gunther,
and playing baseball
with your slippers on.

We called you Cow Harbor.
You jogged to Pumpernickel Hill,
hoping to reach the waterfront.
In a celebration of community,
on a 10K run,
you placed 21!

Famous or unknown
a tale is sewn
of certain allure,
from hill to harbor
from cove to court...
You are, Northport!

Dove's Long Island (1940)

I, too, know these north shore erratics,
these rocks the size of elephants.
Perhaps you, too, also learned about them
in middle school geology, Pleistocene
deposits dropped by a receding behemoth.
Perhaps you also have walked the Caumsett bluffs
have gazed at Target Rock, are part of
the north shore's story, submerged in salty seas,
a piece of sea glass, smoothed by its tides.
Arthur Dove's look like magical eggs, beauties basking
in the glow of a late summer beach day.
The shore is jagged but the rocks are round.
Like elephants, they never forget.
Like Whitman, they know the earth remains broken
only to those who remain broken.
Like me, they don't stray any more.

By Jesse Curran **Artwork by Nayyar Iqbal**

In Loving Memory

Unseen and unheard but always near, so loved so missed, and so very dear

Widow

by Barbara Southard

There was nothing else to be lost,
a certain peace settling over her
like soft dove wings brushing against
the filaments of light that contained her.

Breaking through the clouds, doves gave
one last dip of their wings—a final farewell—
leaving her free to wander toward the lake
where the swans raised their young

or visit Paris and have tea with angels carved from
stone, who offered nothing but the sound of wind
blowing through trees, soft rustle
of dried leaves brushing against new-grown grass.

Artwork by Silvia Maria Rey

The Song of Ganymede

By Luke Briner

Artwork by Deidre Elzer-Lento

I.
I sing of Love and Love attained,
From worldly loneliness detained
To ravished Height of Heavenly embrace,
Brought up by God-inspired flight
So won through his affectioned sight
Of mortal Virtue's hard-acquired grace.
By such Assumption was I made high Jove's beloved thrall
And glad attendant of Olympus' immortal Hall.

II.
Hear now of how I was before:
Meandering that hazy shore
Which Phoebus greeted early in his blaze;
Although by scion's blood its heir,
I felt as if a stranger there,
And on more lofty birthright set my gaze;
For while in common fondness joined to my familiar sire,
A Union with some greater Parent yet was my desire.

III.
I tended then unto my flock,
Unruly brood of Nature's stock
Which only by the staff went not astray;
By that ennobling toil sought I
To prove unto to the distant Sky
My merit to be freed from th'earthly fray.
So hoping, so essaying, and so fixed in high repine
Did I outstretch my aching, prostrate heart to the Divine.

IV.
And then I was by new sense struck,
As though by eagle's talons plucked
As prey submissive from the lowly grass;
No fitful breeze of Aeolus
Or Dæmon tutelar was this,
But Presence of true Otherwordly class.
By Godly Inspiration was I then, in great amaze,
Upswept forthwith from gloom terrene t'ward new World's jocund blaze.

V.
I higher rose than any peak:
Parnassus, where the Sibyls speak
The words of Heaven unto its lost own,
Or Ida blessed, on Cretan isle,
Which Rhea made the domicile
Of my Lord ere he claimed his native Throne;
Those summits seemed to point toward a higher summit still
And urge me to chase the Beloved with more earnest will.

VI.
Soon I had vaulted o'er the Sun
As a triumphant Phaëton
Who earned Supernal sanction thus to rise
By Hubris not but spirit poor
And ardent longing to adore
That kindred Light scarce flashed before my eyes;
So by Empyric wing I flew 'bove each enmattered Sphere
And scraped the primum mobile where Kosmic turns inhere.

VII.
Yet as I gazed upon the Whole,
Work of the Universal Soul,
A Whole far greater was revealed to me:
That Presence shed its pluméd form
Which it to me before had worn
And burst into the Heav'nly Apogee.
The sudden Transformation lifted me, with it entire,
From Hylic bond to that Beyond to which I did aspire.

VIII.
O long-lost Joy now pure and free!
O All-Transcendent Ecstasy!
How can I with these mortal words covey
The Unity Empyrean
And Consolation held therein
Imparted unto me that blesséd day?
At once, at last, did I in that Apotheosis high
Find an Ambrosial balm for every earth-exacted sigh.

IX.
There is in this Elysium
All Being in its perfect Sum
Resounding in a grand polyphony;
I melted in its serenade
And felt my self begin to fade
Before the Beauty that enveloped me.
In Bacchic exultation, drunk with Love, I was led t'ward
My highest télos, the embrace of my Eternal Lord.

X.
He held me to his bosom tight,
And there, at the end of my flight,
I poured out my entire life to him;
I was myself his nec'trous wine
And consort made henceforth Divine,
A homecoming glad from excursion grim.
By noble spirit and above-set mind have I thus won
A perfect Union with my God, no longer two but One.

Light in a Darkened Dreamscape - Virginia Mallon, 2023

Sleepless in January
By Emily-Sue Sloane

The downspout drips worry
across night's frozen canvas
the mind's gathered wool
snags on fences unmended
where sheep wander uncounted

Wind rattles rafters
enough to peel roof tiles from plywood
for a sleigh ride over the eaves

The sky rumbles with a plane's
late-night farewell
and the last train out of the city
races past with a whistled wave
to closed gates at empty crossings

The furnace shudders awake
to pump warmth through rusty pipes
as the TV springs to life
blue glow beckoning
like a searchlight from a distant star
driving endless internal chatter
into the shadows

Artwork by Marilyn Barker

Growing Up Grumman
By Tara Lamberti

The Man in the Moon isn't made of cheese, as young children like to believe.
It's much more magical than that.
He's a humble southern man who sat silently with his Mississippi kin
as the shuttle streaked across the sky, never telling any of his siblings
he'd had a hand in making history. Mom was a 19-year-old hippie in 1969,
unimpressed by metal alloys and theodolites. But standing on the banks of the river
she kept Grampa's secret. When Apollo 11 soared as far as the eye could see – above
the trees, above the clouds, above my father in the jungles of Vietnam, above the
atmosphere, above the world's expectations - she just wished for him to come home.
The Lunar Module allowed the astronauts safe passage from orbit to the Moon's
surface and back. A Chinook allowed Dad one last safe mission before he returned to
American soil. He later joined the team to work on F14s.
My bedroom door was covered with Tomcat stickers. Anytime, Baby…!
Mom and I were Grumman's Girls. Raised knowing our fathers were doing
Big Things. Top Secret things. Really cool things.
Alas, many of the stories that were shared slid through a child's ears, especially mine
at that age. I was eager to dance and play make-believe, not hearing then that it was
my father and grandfather who were the true dreamers.
No, the Man in the Moon isn't made of cheese.
Long Islanders know he's the spirit of generations of Grumman workers,
inspiring us to turn dreams into things,
like a simple plaque affixed to remnants of the LEM
238,855 miles away from home,
"Made in Bethpage, New York"

I Cannot Live Without Magic
by Diana Poulos-Lutz

I cannot live without magic -
the way tiny little soap bubbles dance
around the kitchen as my hands
wash dishes
making rainbow colors like
little angels that smile;
or the fish crow in my yard
calling a call I haven't yet heard;
or most simply the feel of tall trees
close to me, the way it feels
to let in their silent,
wise grandeur and muted aliveness;
the way a large flock of dunlin surround
me in their patterned chaos
and mild sounds
at the beach in the middle
of a cold winter;
and the way whole and broken
washed-up shells speak
stories to my heart.
I cannot live without finding magic
everywhere I am.

Artwork by Jan Guarino

Heaven Has A Dock

by James P. Wagner (Ishwa) Illustrated by Emily Eisen

I glide across the blue as I paddle,
Right side, left side, back and forth,
Floating further towards Northport Harbor...

The water
giving the world a different feel...
And look... And sound... And smell.

Navigating through the anchored sailboats,
I see the kids at the playground,

The retired men playing chess,
A young couple having a picnic...
Perhaps a first date

As the sun rays shine down,   And touch the edge of the harbor...
Guiding me further in towards this little paradise,
I know without a doubt... That heaven has a dock.

Dreams of Kharkiv

Bombs whistling in the night air
Portend explosions to come
We search our parent's faces for calm

And find none

My lyal'ka, Tanya stares back at me,
Her eyes of blue fixed
Her rouged cheeks and simple smile
A constant in this unpredictable night

More whistling

"Tanya, the gods are playing, not to worry
They will stop and put their toys away,
I will put on some tea and we'll visit"

More whistling

The cups rattle,
We stare at each other
And talk of the weather

By Nicole Baccon
Artwork by Mariann Megna

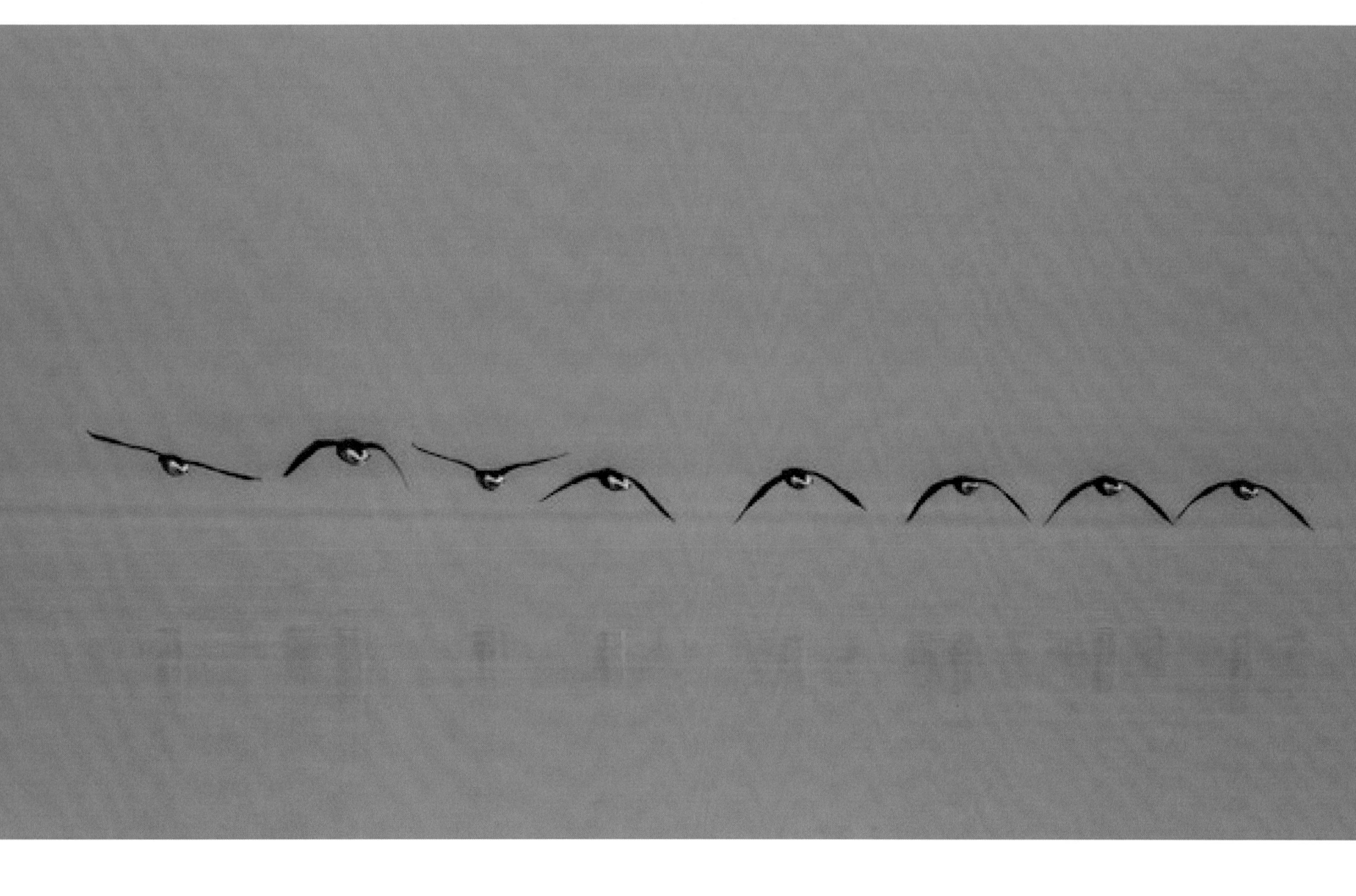

AN OLD FISHING VILLAGE AT DAWN

By George Wallace   Artwork by Nancy Panicucci-Roma

There is a time of day
in the earth's remembered stillness
when the sun breaks hazy over the left shoulder
of the oversized remains of an industrial building
and geese hold steady to their pre-flight positions,
forming up in memory of previous migrations
out across the flat gray harbor.
A time of day when fish by the dozens,
you can hardly believe it, come flipping
out of the meager, almost expressionless,
face of what many in these parts
consider to be dead water. Guess again!
Between the semi-yachts and the last true
fishing boats, before the swirl of oil
and suburban commotion can spoil
the morning, a whole school of fishes,
predators themselves at the moment,
and some of them quite full-bodied
for harbor dwellers, break water
and in such numbers that a seagull,
which had been floating peacefully
somewhere mid-harbor, is suddenly
compelled to take shelter on a pylon
close to shore. It is at times like these
that I walk home with the Sunday paper
and warm rolls tucked under one arm,
encouraged by the continued presence
of two pigeons pecking their way
down Main Street, and this unexpected
communication of life from the harbor
and am content, by God, to ignore
the sun's weak performance in the October sky.

The Magic of Poetry
by Darren Sardelli

A poem can describe
all the things that you like,
like hitting a baseball
or riding a bike,
like painting a picture
or running a race,
like picking a flower
or floating through space.

A poem can be filled with
your thoughts and ideas,
the things you imagine,
your dreams and your fears,
your friends and your family,
your teachers in school,
the games that you play
in a park or a pool..

A poem can tell stories
of dragons and knights,
the hardworking heroes
who fought for your rights,
amazing adventures,
incredible deeds,
a magical wizard
with magical seeds.

A poem can surprise you
with hair raising facts.
A poem can be peaceful
to help you relax.
A poem can have hermit crabs,
dolphins, and fish.
A poem can be simply
whatever you wish.

Artwork by Sebastian Ramirez

Come Follow, Follow Me

By Kristen Memoli

Artwork by Joan Martorana

Come follow, follow me, out beyond where the path leads, over the edge of the broken trail, deep into the embrace of the woods. The soil and leaves lie thick under our feet and give way just enough to memorize our steps, but only for a moment.

Come follow, follow me, where the sparrow sings deep in the brush. His sweet serenade is a reminder that there is joy in the flora. Watching from atop his green and golden perch, he is romancing us with a song that is meant to warn the fauna: "They. Are. Here."

Come follow, follow me, through the thorny wild roses, under dignified fallen trees that lean precariously on their stronger siblings, offering new life in the form of death and decay. The red-headed woodpecker and chipmunk find safety in the woody skeleton while worms devour the heartwood.

Come follow, follow me, to a place where we can sit upon an unexplained tree stump, too jagged to have met its fate at the tooth of a saw but too smooth to be from a recent break. Perhaps years of rain have worked the wood like a fine carpenter's hand, creating a private resting spot for us under the canopy of leaves and sunshine.

Come follow, follow me, where I can reach into the soil, smelling the pungency of billions of unseen creatures edging their way under my fingernails. Come follow, follow me, but NEVER tell anyone where I go to hide; where I go to be among those who can't speak words, yet converse with all of my senses; where I go in silent retreat to listen with bated breath to the stories of the forest.

Now and Again

by Kelly J. Powell   Artwork by Mary Jane Tenerelli

Your hometown is an archipelago of hopes
and dreams and wrong numbers and failed

romance you wish you could be a seagull
if that were not an Armageddon of a loftier kind

and it is the loneliness that will take you in the end
and in the beginning all things are possible

teaspoons and silverware all around you numbering
your dead and you still go on maybe not the gift

it would appear to be being the survivor, the widow,
the caregiver the nurse the cook the bottle washer

and memory keeper s 2nd wife turning tragedy
into strategy no simple art and the lion in my heart

roars and roars and the car won't start and the kids
are grown and dishes in the sink was the only good rule

and the only rule dandelion chains and misery
become her the curse of the Irish always longing

for home while they are in it full force of it
the embrace of it the sweetest of excruciating coming

to brew with the tea we don't drink tea here even
though there are a thousand brands out there

every micro leaf of it waiting for company that comes
too often but not enough enlightening us frightening

us visits from strangers nurses gardeners plumbers
electricians installing gutter s windows doorstops

train stops whistleblowers orange pickers scarf
knitters blustering gale snowdrifts of the mind

going south for the winter answer the door
opportunity keeps calling and going to your full

voicemail Check the mail go to sleep perchance
to dream to heal to love and honor and live in the

eternity of now and then and again
and again and again

#1483 (Northport, 1996)

By Douglas G. Swezey

Artwork by Vivian Pollack

We used to see second run movies
For two bucks on a Friday night
With our group of friends
Huddling close in our seats
After filing through the sticky rows
And the smell of heavy butter on
Stale popcorn permeating the theatre
Afterwards, wander down Main
To the deli on the corner of
Woodbine, grab a Snapple
And sit out on the patio behind
Laughing and shooting the breeze
We'd head over to see the new releases
On vinyl at Tracks on Wax, pause at the
Acupuncturist's house set back a bit
Adorned in orange & brown, cross back over
To the Presbyterian Church and head back
Passing the other churches, past Union
Where my mom parked illegally
By the apartments, while taking me to see

Oscar the barber for my first haircuts
Past the crowd of smokers outside Gunthers
See if we knew anyone working at Lics
Until we got back to Constitution Square
Then hang out at the Gazebo late into the night
Overlooking the harbour, it's tide lapping up
Against the docks under fluorescent lights
Maybe play King of the Hill on the softest
Grass in the village at the corner of Bayview &
Highland, across from the park, trying to do
So quietly, before the homeowners would hear
Then loiter on the swings in the new
Playground, maybe mosey over to the docks
And stare out at Centerport before heading
Back to the parking lot to find our cars
And head home, finally, in the wee hours of
The Northport night, where we had the
Village to ourselves, no one to bother us
But the impending sunrise of the next day

Artwork by Oksana Danziger

A Singular Spectator

By Joan Amato

Singular little dandelion
Rises up to kiss the sun
Stretching its buttercup bud
Through unyielding earth

It knows not the weather
Or if the sun will shine
Or if raindrops will fall
Nourishing its bloom

This butterweed surges up
Through endless layers of loam
Emerges through soggy soil
Remnants of winter's slush

She shows her might
Rooting to reveal her smiling blossom
Only to be gone the next day's dawning
Recessed into the cold earth
To await the sunshine again
That channels her out of her nook

Sitting upright in her little patch
Her honeyed face smiles to the sun
As if to say I am here once again
Shower me with your warmth.

ARTIST AND POET BIOS

Joan Amato (Poet) has taught writing in various colleges in Ohio, Maine and Long Island. Her first love is poetry, which has been published in a variety of small presses and journals including the Suffolk County Poetry Review, Avocet, Neighborhood Newspapers, Long Island Sounds: 2023 An Anthology of Poetry From Maspeth to Montauk and Beyond, and The Long Islander.

Nicole Baccon (Poet) has dedicated her working life to the medical field but has always participated, enjoyed and supported the arts. She looks for opportunities like this one to try her hand at a challenge. She sees this as an opportunity to broaden one's network of collaborators who share a similar mindset. She is an avid reader, seeking adventure and new experiences. She grew up in Queens, the most multicultural place on earth.

Marilyn Barker (Artist) is a self-taught artist, crafter, sometimes poet. Born October 2nd, 1940, Englewood, NJ. Participating member of the Firefly Artists Gallery, Main Street, Northport, member Huntington Harbormasters Senior painters. Graduated Northport High School, Suffolk Community College, St. Joseph's College. "My art is lively and colorful with a touch of humor."

Luke Briner (Poet) is a senior at St. John's College, Annapolis. He hopes to pursue a career in philosophy and writing after graduating

Paula Curci (Poet) is the 2022-24 Nassau County Poet Laureate is a spoken word poet, broadcaster and retired school counseling educator. For nearly two decades she has hosted and produced Calliope's Corner - The Place Where Poets and Songwriters Meet, an award-winning radio show. Her poetry has been featured in a multitude of anthologies: The Nassau County Poet Laureate Society Review, The PPA Literary Review, Nomads Choir, Bards Annual, The Vault's Soul Fountain, Whispers and Shouts, Writing Outside the Lines, LunaSea Press Hysteria and The National Association of Poetry Therapists' Poet's Process, among others. Paula is a co-founding member of The Acoustic Poets Network© and her Posics ™ style poetry is found on streaming services. Through The APN she has released three spoken word albums. Paula is frequently found reciting her poetry at Performance Poetry Association events and other venues across Long Island. She currently resides in Long Beach, New York.

Jesse Curran (Poet) is a poet, essayist, scholar, and teacher who lives in Northport. Her essays and poems have appeared in dozens of literary journals including About Place, Ruminate, After the Art, Allium, Blueline, and Saltfront. She teaches in the Department of English at SUNY Old Westbury. www.jesseleecurran.com

Oksana Danziger (Artist) is a natural born creator with a passion for textile art. She thrives as a freelance textile artist, collaborating with various renowned studios such as Printfolio, Design Works International, and Group Four. Oksana has an impressive clientele, including esteemed brands like Tommy Bahama, Ann Taylor, and Gap. In addition to her artistic pursuits, Oksana shares her expertise by teaching at the Nassau Art Museum and conducting workshops in schools through esteemed organizations such as the Huntington Arts Council, Art Guild of Port Washington, Gallery North, and CEED (a non-profit educational organization). She also served as an adjunct professor in the surface design department at The Fashion Institute of Technology (FIT).

Emily Eisen (Artist) has lived in her dear hometown of Northport for 36 years, teaching and creating art, writing, singing, song-writing and loving the creative community of kindred spirits. She loved illustrating James P. Wagner's poem Heaven Is A Dock because she feels this, too! Every season Northport village and harbor is the vortex that brings everyone such beauty, spirit and connection to nature and each other. "I'm grateful to be living here with my treasured community."

Deidre Elzer-Lento (Artist) is an accomplished photographer who enjoys photographing, manipulating and sharing her images. She teaches photography, lectures and judges photographic exhibitions. Deidre's work resides in the permanent collections of museums and businesses. She has been published in books, newspapers, and magazines. She calls Long Island's North Shore home.

Jan Guarino (Artist) loves everything about watercolors, painting and teaching the beauty and fun of this medium. She is capable of capturing the essence and beauty of a variety of different subjects. Her paintings are for sale on her website and at the Firefly Gallery in our village. She is a graduate of the Fashion Institute of Technology. janguarinofineart.com

Nayyar Iqbal (Artist) is an American-Pakistani artist working with bold colors and strokes. Her passion for painting revolves around street scenes and old buildings of cities balanced with the images of daily life. She feels proud to exhibit her work in her studio. Being able to communicate the beauty she perceives through her paintings is a great blessing to her. She looks forward to her future endeavors in exhibiting her work.

Kate Kelly (Artist) was a founding member of the Northport Arts Coalition and is active in the arts community both as a visual artist and poet. In 2005 she was recognized as a New York State Woman of Distinction. Her poetry has been published in numerous small press magazines and online publication, as well as in her own books. Her visual art has appeared in countless galleries and exhibits, including fotofoto Gallery, the Huntington Arts Council gallery, Alfred Van Loen Gallery, SNUUC Foyer Gallery, the Custer Institute, Smithtown Arts Council, and Stepping Stone Gallery, to name a few. She has served as an associate editor of the online poetry magazine, Poetry Bay, and has curated several exhibits for the Art League of Long Island and the Northport Arts Coalition.

Tara Lamberti (Poet) lives on the South Shore of Long Island with her newly-wedded husband. She believes writing is a special kind of magic. She has been published in numerous Bards Annual anthologies, and Oberon. "Growing Up Grumman" won first place in the 2019 Long Island Fair poetry competition.

Virginia Mallon (Artist) is an artist working in paint and photography. Her work contemplates religious, historic, and mythological women, personal histories, the psychological and political undercurrents of contemporary society. www.VirginiaMallon.com

Joan Martorana (Artist) started exploring art at an early age. From paper art to recycled sculptures. It was when Joan experienced working in oils that her love of painting evolved. After retiring from teaching, Joan devoted her time to watercolors, developing her skills of capturing the beauty of nature around her.

Mariann Megna (Artist) is a multi-media artist working in watercolor, oil paint and glass. Mariann studied at the Art Studio of the Hamptons with Ben Fenske, James Dada Albinson, and Tim McGuire among others. She also studied at The Artists League of NY in Manhattan. Mariann is a singer/songwriter currently performing at the Allegria Hotel in Long Beach NY with four original albums recorded.

Kristen Memoli (Poet), a psychologist and self-taught artist and writer, is inspired by contradiction: light versus dark, life versus decay, joy versus heartache. Her multimedia pieces often feature text which helps convey more depth than images/objects alone. Memoli's first book, The Secret Soul of Things, is her most expansive project to date.

Nancy Panicucci-Roma (Artist) is an avid photographer with a deep passion for nature, wildlife, and humanitarian causes. She is dedicated to capturing images that showcase stunning natural beauty as well as those which evoke powerful emotions, allowing viewers to connect with both the world around us and the human spirit within. Nancy loves sharing her images, inviting others to experience her world through her lens. Thanks to her photography skills, Nancy has formed enduring connections with individuals from all walks of life.

Vivien Pollack (Artist) began her art career as a Textile Designer, designing for the textile print industry in NYC, creating original designs that were sold to manufacturers. She has since exhibited many award-winning paintings in galleries and shows. Besides painting on silk, she works with oils and pastels.

Diana Poulos-Lutz (Poet) has an M.A., M.Phil. in Politics. Diana's poems have won several local and international awards. Diana's first book, Time to Rise, was published in 2020. Her second book, I Walk On, was published in 2023. Diana's poetry is inspired by her love of nature, mindfulness, equality, and empowerment.

Kelly J. Powell (Poet) is a poet native to Long Island and a graduate of SUNY Binghamton's Creative Writing Program in 1988. She runs a reading series at bj spoke gallery in Huntington and has performed widely on Long Island and NYC. Her book Posthumously Yours from Local Gems Press and Amazon.

Sebastian Ramirez (Artist) Sebastian Ramirez is an illustrator from Austin, Texas. He likes to draw fantasy characters and creatures heavily influenced by The Witcher and Lovecraft but other realms of interest are more than welcome. His previous work history includes logo design and album cover art.

Silvia Maria Rey (Artist) Silvia María Rey is an educator, author, and award-winning artist from New York. Originally from Havana, Cuba, she immigrated to the United States in 1961 with her parents and brother. She attended Cardinal Spellman HS where she received her first formal instruction in the fine arts cementing her love for the visual arts. She received a Bachelor of Fine Arts degree from Herbert H. Lehman College. She went on to receive several advanced certificates and degrees in the field of education focusing on the literacy needs of bilingual students and second language learners.

Darren Sardelli (Poet) is an award-winning poet and author. His poems have been featured on Radio Disney, in popular books on the Scholastic Book List, and appear in 28 children's books in the U.S. and U.K. Darren visits schools, where he makes poetry fun. For more information, please visit www.LaughAlotPoetry.com

Emily-Sue Sloane (Poet) is an award-winning poet whose work appears in many journals and anthologies. She is the author of full-length collection We Are Beach Glass (2022) and chapbook Disconnects and other Broken Threads (The Poetry Box, 2024). She lives in Huntington Station, NY, with her wife, singer-songwriter Linda Sussman. https://EmilySueSloane.com

Barbara Southard (Poet) is a visual artist and writer living in Miller Place, New York. The titles of her three books are: Remember, published in 2008, Time & Space, published in 2020, and Long Island Poems, published 2022. She served as Suffolk County Poet Laureate from 2019-2021.

Douglas G. Swezey (Poet) received his B.A. in English and Art History from Stony Brook University in 2004. He's written as a journalist for many weekly newspapers, served as the Managing Editor of Government Food Services Magazine, and is the author of Stony Brook University: Off The Record. He currently serves on the boards of the Long Island Poetry Collective, The North Sea Poetry Scene, and the Bard's Initiative. He is an Associate Editor of Poetry Bay and was the host of the Long Island Poetry Collective's Reading Series.

Mary Jane Tenerelli (Artist) began taking pictures in March of 2020. Her work consists mostly of flora, both full bloom and dying, as well as abstract landscapes or dreamscapes. Her lifelong love of poetry informs her photography. Her work can be seen on her Instagram page @maryjanetenerelli.

James P Wagner (Ishwa) (Poet) is the publisher for Local Gems Press, founder and president of the Bards Initiative, and National Beat Poet Laureate emeritus. He has edited over 120 poetry anthologies, and is the owner-operator of the Dog-Eared Bards Book Shop in East Northport.

George Wallace (Poet) is writer in residence at the Walt Whitman Birthplace, author of 39 chapbooks of poetry, and first poet laureate of Suffolk County. A writing professor at Pace University in NYC, he is a prominent member of the performance scene and travels worldwide to share his work. George has won numerous international awards, including most recently being named poet of the year at the Boao International Poetry Festival in Hainan China (2022). He is editor of Poetrybay and Walt's Corner, co-editor of Great Weather for Media and Long Island Quarterly, curator of Poets Building Bridges, and in 2022 edited the Blue Lights Press anthology NYC FROM THE INSIDE.

www.ingramcontent.com/pod-product-compliance
Lightning Source LLC
Chambersburg PA
CBRC101521070526
44585CB00010B/175